My Toddler Talks

Strategies and Activities to
Promote Your Child's
Language Development

Kimberly Scanlon, M.A., CCC-SLP

Table of Contents

Acknowledgements

I would like to thank all my clients, previous and current, for inspiring me to write this book. Watching your children blossom and grow has been so rewarding. I consider myself blessed to have the opportunity to work with such caring and dedicated parents. Thank you for making my "work" days so enjoyable.

Completing this book would not have been possible without the loving support of my husband Ryan and my parents, who always encouraged me to sit down and stay with it. Thank you for keeping me motivated when I needed it most.

Last but not least, thank you to my good friend and fellow speech-language pathologist Jolene Lawton, for so carefully reading and editing my book. Thanks for your attention to detail and for painstakingly correcting any punctuation or style errors. You're the best!

About the Author

KIMBERLY O. SCANLON, MA, CCC-SLP

Kimberly is a New Jersey licensed speech pathologist and is nationally certified by the American Speech and Hearing Association (ASHA). She is a creative thinker and a passionate therapist who believes that children should have fun in therapy. Kimberly has had the opportunity to hone her skills by working in various settings serving all ages, populations, and disorders. She is a two-time recipient of ASHA's award for continuing education (ACE), which formally recognizes professionals who have demonstrated their commitment to lifelong learning by earning seven CEUs (seventy hours) within a thirty-six-month period. She graduated from Rutgers University with a bachelor of science and earned her master of arts in Communication Disorders from Montclair State University. In addition to writing, Kimberly is busy running her private practice, Scanlon Speech Therapy, LLC, in New Jersey. If you are interested in learning more speech and language tips, techniques, and activities, please visit her website, www.scanlonspeech.com. Kimberly lives with her wonderful husband, Ryan, their delightful daughter, Kerrigan, and their very cute but mischievous chocolate Labrador retriever, Barney.

Disclaimer

If you have genuine concerns regarding a child's speech, language, and play skills, please consult a licensed and certified speech-language pathologist for guidance. This book is not meant to replace speech therapy. For those children in speech therapy, it can be used in conjunction with the recommendations of the treating speech-language pathologist. Please be advised that Kimberly Scanlon, MA, CCC-SLP, is a licensed speech-language pathologist. Kimberly may recommend products, toys, and activities, which, if properly used, may be educational in nature to help adults work with children to improve their language skills. Kimberly hereby disclaims any and all liability occurring as a result of any alleged or actual claims against her as a result of the usage of these products. Please be aware and be guided accordingly that the products recommended by Kimberly may contain small parts which may cause a choking hazard, and they should never be used by children unless under the strict supervision of an adult. Kimberly does not guarantee speech/language progress or that children will want to engage in play with their parents and/or do the recommended activities. This book is not intended to, nor could it take the place of the advice and/or intervention from, a physician, speech-language pathologist, or early-childhood provider who has evaluated your child in person. It is not speech-language therapy, nor is it a professional assessment of any child's speech and language skills.

Freeze!

Stop right there. Before you even think about skipping the introduction and going straight to the play routines, let me strongly suggest that you read the introduction first. Since there is so much valuable information in the introduction, I even recommend reading it more than once. Enjoy and happy reading. I wish you much success!

Introduction

Are you interested in jumpstarting your toddler's speech? Would you like to learn some strategies to help your child talk? If so, then you are reading the right book! This book has been written to help parents and caregivers facilitate the communication and play skills of their toddlers. My play activities and techniques are straightforward and easy for nonprofessionals to implement. It is my goal that readers will become so comfortable using the learned strategies that they will apply them throughout the day with their children. Educators, speech-language pathologists, and others working with or interacting with toddlers will also find this book helpful. The activities were written primarily for children aged eighteen to thirty-six months old, but younger or older children can also benefit, depending on their skills, personality, and maturity. For simplicity, the term *parent* will be used to include any adult who wishes to participate in fun play routines and to learn language-enhancing strategies. The terms *toddler* and *toddlers* will also be used to represent the targeted age group. The male gender pronouns (he, him, and his) will be used to keep things succinct.

Play

Toddlers are a very curious bunch. Most are hands-on and enjoy exploring their environment and discovering new toys and objects. All this curiosity helps to drive their learning. Play is an essential learning tool for toddlers and is very important to their overall development and cognition. In addition to helping them communicate and socialize, play further develops problem solving, attention, hand-eye coordination, visual perceptual, and fine motor skills. Research shows that certain play skills, language structures, and specific cognitive concepts occur simultaneously during the same stage of development. For instance, for a child to engage in pretend play, he has to have the ability to understand that objects can be used symbolically to represent other objects. At the same time, he has to have enough language to engage in social dialogue and negotiation to make the pretend play meaningful. For more information on how play relates to language, please see **Appendix D: How Play Relates to Language**.

A child's language and cognitive development is additionally boosted when an adult appropriately plays and engages with him. Furthermore, play helps to strengthen the bonds between parent and child. This is because play allows a parent to enter a child's world. Play provides a relaxed, secure context to offer parental assistance and guidance.

Over the years, I have educated many parents and adults on how to effectively engage and play with toddlers. I have discovered that some adults are not comfortable playing with toddlers, or they are not confident in their own play skills. Either the play is too simple or, more often, too advanced. The latter may happen because some adults have very high expectations of toddlers' abilities. Parents also have to be careful not to be overly controlling during play. When this occurs, the benefits of play are greatly diminished because the adult takes away the child's ability to be creative and solve problems. For these reasons, I have provided directions on how to facilitate the toddler's independence, creativity, and problem-solving skills. Although my play routines are structured by the adult, the toddler ultimately makes the decisions and leads the way. The adult merely serves as a facilitator.

Routines

When thinking of routines, we tend to think of an order of events occurring in a predictable, set manner. For instance, I have a morning routine. First, I begrudgingly get out of bed, brush my teeth, wash my face, get dressed, and eat breakfast. Having a routine makes tackling the day a bit more tolerable because it provides an organized framework within which to function. For this reason, many adults like to set schedules and develop routines with toddlers. Some of these routines may include getting dressed, participating in regular play dates, preparing and eating meals, joining in circle time at the library, having a set quiet time, and going to bed. These routines tend to occur at certain times of the day.

Research has shown that set routines are very important to a toddler's sense of well-being and growth. Toddlers are happier when they know what to expect because it gives them a sense of security and comfort. This helps them to trust adults and feel more comfortable exploring their environment.

Predictable routines also encourage learning. Social skills such as waving hello and saying goodbye are routines that some adults quickly introduce to young ones. Routines help some toddlers make transitions between activities and events. For instance, if an adult rings a bell, sings a song, or claps his hands to signal that it's almost time to go or to change activities, then a child will be ready to make that transition. These routines do not have to be very rigid to be effective. In other words, you don't always have to do the same thing day in and day out. Flexibility and variations are fine as long as the child knows what will ultimately happen in the end.

· ·

My play routines are structured by the adult, but the toddler is the one who makes the decisions and leads the way. The adult merely serves as a facilitator.

· ·

Play Routines

These two fundamental concepts of play and routine have been combined to form play routines. A play routine is established when participation in a fun activity follows a predictable pattern or sequence. Having play routines can facilitate the communication and play skills of toddlers. This book has twenty-five fun play routines specifically designed to enhance a toddler's speech and language skills.

I have designed these play routines to become a part of a toddler's typical everyday routine. The play becomes predictable enough to provide a framework for learning language and increasing communication. Also, I have structured the play routines so that the toddler can learn what to expect each time. Structuring predictability into play helps him to initiate communication because he can anticipate what will happen next.

Lastly, many toddlers tend to enjoy some repetition in their play. What may seem like the same old boring routine to adults is exciting to toddlers. In my work, I have found that when toddlers experience success with a toy or activity, they like to recreate that experience. This is because doing so increases their confidence and sense of well-being. If a toddler is not talking yet, have him participate in something that is easy to do and creates the feeling of success. Repeating a highly desirable activity with the toddler while encouraging him to follow a routine helps to increase his motivation, which can facilitate language acquisition.

> The toddler may follow a direction, identify a picture, or use a gesture or sign before saying words or verbalizing his intentions.

Setting Expectations

Increasing a child's ability to initiate communication is a desirable goal. However, a language-delayed child or a late talker may first become responsive to communication bids before initiating dialogue. For instance, the toddler may follow directions (e.g., "Stop it" or "Come here"), identify pictures, or even use gestures or motions before saying words or verbalizing his intentions. This is because comprehension generally precedes production.

Additionally, toddlers often need to imitate and repeat spoken words and phrases before spontaneously applying them on their own. So don't be shocked when you notice that your toddler is parroting everything you say. This happens even if he doesn't understand the words you are using or what you are saying.

Toddlers' first words also tend to be rooted in certain contexts and situations. For instance, the child may begin saying "dog" only when he sees or hears his neighbor's dog, but not when he sees or hears other dogs. This is because the child has not yet fully understood the application of that word. He understands a word based on its specific context. Eventually, the toddler's understanding grows, and he learns to extend the word to multiple contexts and different situations.

A word can be defined as "a sound sequence that symbolizes meaning and can stand alone" (Hoff, 2005 p. 422). Therefore, a dog barking, a baby crying, or a cat meowing may convey meaning, but these sounds are not symbols, and therefore they are not words. If your child is not yet combining words or saying phrases on his own, try tracking his or her vocabulary. If you are interested in measuring your toddler's word growth, please see **Appendix A: Track Your Toddler's Vocabulary Growth** or visit the iTunes store to download the app *My Toddler Talks: Word Tracker*.

Lastly, it's not realistic to assume that a child who has not been speaking will start saying phrases or sentences overnight. This can happen, but it is rare. Typically, children need to have a certain number of words in their repertoire before they can start combining words into phrases and sentences. A general rule of thumb is that children have fifty words in their repertoire before combining words. This is because when they get to this fifty-word benchmark, many children then usually have a "word spurt," and their talking takes off. However, word spurts may not occur with all children. Some children's language development may follow a more linear pattern, and their vocabulary may grow at a more constant rate regardless of how many words they have in their repertoire.

How to Use This Book

1. **Incorporate a set playtime into the child's daily routine.**

   Select a time when the child is well rested, fed, changed, and available for learning. This should also be an appropriate time for the adult; refrain from scheduling this time when one might be distracted by morning news shows, afternoon talk shows, evening sitcoms, or miscellaneous errands and chores. A thirty- to forty-five-minute period dedicated to playtime should suffice, depending on your schedule. If you have more time and your toddler wants to play longer, then by all means, continue to play! Once a time has been selected, keep to this schedule, as routines are important to a child's well-being. If you need help creating a schedule to organize your toddler's daily routine, please see **Appendix B: Making Routines for Your Toddler**.

2. **Follow the toddler's lead during play.**

   Although this book provides fun activities with play routines included, it's important to follow the child's lead and allow him to make choices. The main goal should not be to complete an activity systematically, but rather to take turns and be responsive to the child's actions and utterances. Think of your toddler as a communicative partner. If you find that you are doing all the talking, then something is amiss. Focus on sharing and balancing the communication exchange. Do not become too focused on following every step in the routine. These directions are meant to be a helpful guide. Be flexible and allow the child to take charge too.

3. **Modify the play routines as needed.**

   You know your child best. I may be the expert when it comes to speech and language, but parents are the experts when it comes to their children. For this reason, my play routines can be easily adjusted to make them particularly motivating for your toddler. If one routine seems too basic or too challenging, you can simplify a step, give more or less support, or skip it entirely and revisit that routine later. My play routines are not meant to be exhaustive, nor are they meant to be strictly interpreted. I only stress that you implement play routines that are somewhat repetitive and predictable. Following my instructions may make this goal easier to achieve. It will also allow the child to learn a certain concept and know what to expect.

4. **Start and end with something easy, but challenge him a little in the middle.**

   As mentioned before, routines follow a sequence. My play routines have a beginning, a middle, and an end. Typically, I start my sessions with something that is easy or very motivating for the child. Then, as time progresses (by the middle of the session), I challenge the child with something new or different. As the session ends, I finish on a positive note by having the child participate in something that he or she is good at and has been successful doing. Be mindful to end a play routine when you sense that the child is losing interest. I also like to sing songs while cleaning up to make this a more enjoyable process. In my experience, most toddlers enjoy cleaning up and putting things away because they like to help and model adults! Please see **Appendix C: Songs to End Routines** for my three favorite clean-up songs.

5. **Keep it simple and short.**

   For many activities, I've included sounds, words, or phrases to elicit speech and language from the child. Gauge what you think he can imitate or understand. For the child who is nonverbal or not yet talking, make sounds such as *moo* for a cow, *choo choo* for a train, or *woof woof* for a dog, or you can say single words or very short and concrete phrases. If the child is only imitating one word when you say two or three, do not use five- or six-word sentences with the expectation that the child will repeat a targeted word; he will have already forgotten what you said!

If you need assistance in picking out potential target words, please see **Appendix E: Common First Words** to guide you. If you find that the child is not imitating anything you are saying or doing, then you must do some troubleshooting. Please see the section titled **Troubleshooting Techniques: What to Do if the Toddler Is Not Imitating You** for more information.

6. **Set goals for your session.**

   Devising goals, such as "Sammy will use one or two words to express her needs and wants," will give you focus and help guide your effort. In **Appendix F: Language Goals**, I have listed several language goals to assist you in choosing and maintaining direction.

7. **Chart your progress.**

   How can you know that you are making progress with your toddler's language? Establish a baseline by asking yourself, "What is my toddler doing now?" Then select goals, and track the specific changes or improvements related to your efforts. Taking these steps will help you stay motivated and know whether your efforts are effective. Check out Appendix G: Progress Chart for guidance.

8. **Have fun!**

   When toddlers are having fun, they want to learn. Praise the process, not just the results.

I have had great success implementing these strategies, and I have effectively used these activities with numerous children throughout the years. It is my sincere hope that you find them useful with your children. However, I cannot guarantee their success, as every child is different, and each reader will implement them to varying degrees using an individualized approach.

Language Modeling Techniques and Elicitation Strategies

Many of the following techniques are well known in the speech therapy circle. Please consult the reference list if you are interested in reading more articles and books related to using these techniques.

1. **Self-talk**

   Talk about what you are doing, seeing, eating, touching, or thinking when your child is present. Narrate your actions - for example, "I'm washing the dishes. Now, I'm drying them. All done. I washed the dishes." Remember to use words and phrases that are age appropriate. Some children may better understand if only one or two words are said, rather than longer phrases or sentences ("washing dishes," "drying dishes," and "all done").

2. **Parallel talk**

   Talk about what the child is doing, seeing, eating, or touching. In other words, narrate what he is doing - for example, "Now Johnny's washing the dishes. He's washing the plate. There, it's clean! All done. Johnny washed the plate."

   ❖ When using self-talk and parallel talk, you are NOT requiring your child to respond to or imitate what you are saying. Please do not have the expectation that your child is automatically going to imitate or repeat you. These techniques simply give your child exposure to language during play and daily routines. This helps toddlers realize that talking during play is fun. If they imitate or repeat you, that's wonderful!

3. Expand

Add grammatically correct information to your child's meaningful yet incomplete utterances. If your child says, "boy run," you could say, "Yes, the boy is running." As you can see, you are adding the missing words. This technique is for children who are speaking but using incomplete sentences.

> ❖ Use this expansion technique in moderation to preserve a natural communicative exchange.

4. Follow the toddler's lead in conversation

Simply put, talk about what your child wants to talk about. If your child is looking at the rain, talk about the rain; if he is looking at the dog, talk about the dog. This includes acknowledging the child's words, phrases, and actions by saying something or doing something. Model or copy his actions, and then repeat and restate what he says. Be responsive to what he does or says, even if it's not a real word. The goal is to increase the child's attention and intentionality.

5. Question a little, not a lot

Don't inundate your child with too many questions. We've all been here before—in tester mode, when we ask questions even though we already know the answer. Children are more intuitive than we often think, and they realize that we are quizzing them. For instance, "Johnny, what's this? What's that? Who's this? Who's that?" With children, questions tend to put them on the spot, limit their responses, and end conversations, ultimately having the opposite effect of what's intended. Remember to balance questions with comments. As a rule of thumb, saying at least three comments before asking one question is usually the best method. This is because dialogue is encouraged in a more natural manner. Refrain from asking closed-ended questions that require yes or no responses (e.g., "Is this red? Is the doll dancing? Are we going to ride the train?").

6. **Pause in anticipation**

   Wait approximately three to five seconds to give your child a chance to respond to what you have asked or said. Show that you are waiting expectantly by raising your eyebrows, smiling, and opening your mouth.

7. **Sentence-completion tasks**

   This technique is best suited for older children, or those who have stronger comprehension skills. Try pairing auditory input with visual or tactile input. For example, while giving him his shirt, say, "Here's your shirt. Put on your _____." Additional prompting may include use of phonemic cues. A phonemic cue is when you give the first sound of the target word. They help children retrieve words and say them quicker. For example, while giving him his shirt, say, "Here's your shirt. Put on your sh_____."

8. **Choices**

   Give the toddler choices: "Do you want to eat crackers or grapes?" or "Do you want the cow or the horse?" Doing so puts indirect pressure on the toddler by presenting him with a concrete choice.

9. **Oops!**

   Forget something essential or skip an important step in a routine. Most toddlers know when a routine has been violated and want to point out the mistake.

   ❖ Give your child cereal, but forget to give him a spoon.

   ❖ Set the table, but skip your child's place setting.

   ❖ Make a mistake by giving him a fork instead of a spoon.

10. **Gestures, pantomime, or silly sounds**

   Use these to help the child understand your intentions. For instance, if you want the ball, point to the ball while saying "ball," or if you know any sign language, sign for the ball. If you want his or her stuffed duck, make the quack-quack motion with your hands (four fingers come together to touch the thumb) while saying "quack quack."

11.Set it up

Don't overly anticipate the needs of the child. Set up a scenario so that the child has to ask for help or assistance. Give him a box or bag you know he can't open, or give him a task you know he will struggle with, so that he will have to ask for your help. This may sound mean, but it isn't!

Since caregiving routines, such as getting dressed, eating, taking a nap, and going to the store, occur on a regular basis, I highly encourage parents to use these techniques during their everyday life.

Troubleshooting Tips: What to Do if the Toddler Is Not Imitating You

There is always the child who does not imitate your words. If you think you are implementing the techniques appropriately, but little Johnny or tiny Tina is not imitating your words, then what should you do? First, try to analyze your interaction with the child. Are you dominating the play and talking too much? It might help to have another family member or friend sit with you and your toddler and observe you. Video-record a play session, and then watch it to see if you have correctly followed the techniques. If you are working with a child that is not your own, you need consent from the parent to video-record!

Remember **_R-A-I-S-E-S_** to help you facilitate your toddler's language learning by incorporating some of the following techniques into your play routines:

1. **_R_educe pressure**

   Minimize the pressure and stress you place on the toddler. Have you been asking too many questions? If so, replace a question with a comment. For instance, instead of saying, "What is this?" while pointing to a picture, talk about what you see in the picture: "I see a big ball." Pause and look at the child. This way you are not confronting the child with a direct question or placing too many demands on him. Keep the play fun and lighthearted if you sense he has started to lose interest or get frustrated.

2. Add support

Provide auditory, visual, and tactile support when needed. Show pictures, point to desired items, use gestures, and amplify sounds and words. For amplification, try using a microphone, a tube, or cardboard roll.

3. Imitate the child

If the child says "woof woof," echo it back to him: "woof woof." This strengthens the connection between the child and adult, and children often get very excited when adults imitate them!

4. Slow it down

Slow down your rate of speech. Toddlers who are beginning to acquire language may not process what you are saying if you say it too quickly. Imagine trying to learn a new language with a teacher who speaks a mile a minute. It's pretty challenging.

5. Exaggerate your intonation

Slow down your rate of speech and use over-exaggerated intonation: "I reeeeeally liiiiiiike this game!"

6. Short and sweet

I've mentioned this before, but it's worth repeating since I've seen many parents speak at a level above their toddler's abilities. If the child is only imitating one word when you say two or three, then do not produce a long-winded five- or six-word sentence with the expectation that the child will repeat a targeted word, because he has already forgotten what you said!

The Do Not List

Think *C-U-T-I-E* to help you remember what NOT to do while playing with *your* cutie!

1. **Correcting your child's communication**

   For example, if your child is pointing to a dog and saying "daw," he should not be corrected by saying, "No, Johnny, that's a dog." For a child who has not begun talking yet, saying "daw" is a good improvement. Encourage and praise any attempts, even if they are weak or unintelligible, by repeating the desired target ("dog!") or praising his attempt: "You're right, Johnny, that's a dog!"

2. **Using too many negatives**

   Avoid too many *no's* and *don'ts.* Plain and simple—negativity is not fun!

3. **Teaching the ABCs**

   If the child is having a slow start in acquiring language, then I don't recommend teaching academically related vocabulary such as numbers, colors, letters, or shapes. It's better to target words that will give meaning and relevancy to his speech; this includes word categories such as actions, objects, locations, and attributes that are most relevant to a child's communication system.

4. **Ignoring your child's interest**

   If your child points to a tree, look at the tree, acknowledge it, and say something about it or expand on what your child said about the tree. Don't begin talking about the weather or the neighbors. Stick to the topic!

5. *Expecting too much too soon*

Acquiring language is a process for some children. Toddlers are young and therefore need lots of opportunities, multiple contexts, and much repetition to acquire new skills. Some toddlers pick up words quickly, while others may take a more gradual approach. Give them time to grow at their own pace. Enjoy this playtime with your toddler, and make sure he feels that you are enjoying it, too, that it's not work or a chore. Toddlers are very perceptive and can tell when others are disappointed.

Some More Tips: The Five Rs

Here are five more tips to help accelerate your toddler's language learning.

❖ **_R_aise it up!**

>   Hold desired objects or toys next to your face so that your child has to look at your face when you're talking. Placement next to your eyes or mouth is fine. For instance, if your toddler wants a cookie, hold the cookie close to your mouth while you say "cookie" so he can watch your lips move.

❖ **_R_einforce**

>   Use natural reinforcers or rewards, such as giving your child a big hug, an extra turn in play, or verbal praise to keep him encouraged.

❖ **_R_espond**

>   If your child said "ba" while pointing to a boat, acknowledge his verbal production by looking at the boat and talking about it. He is interested in that boat, which is why he tried to name it.

❖ **_R_earrange**

>   Manipulate the environment to provide opportunities for communicating with preferred toys or everyday objects. Position favorite toys or desired objects in sight but out of reach. If you know he wants the

fire truck because he plays with it every time he's in his highchair, do not just give it to him. Allow him the opportunity to point to the fire truck and try to name it before readily giving it to him. If he can't say it that's OK, just provide a model question, such as "Fire truck?" or "Do you want the fire truck?" Doing this will give him the opportunity to verbalize his needs and wants.

❖ *Relax and wait…a little*

Give the child enough time to explore and problem solve. Toddlers learn through discovery. Provide them with just enough support so that they can try to figure it out on their own. Try to gauge or anticipate when you need to help them so that they don't get frustrated. How do you know an activity is too challenging or advanced for the child? If the child becomes frustrated, then this may be a sign that he is over-taxed or simply not understanding it. Stop the activity or make it easier if you find that the child is no longer having fun.

Toy Activities

Animal Farm

Materials:

A barn

Farm animals—cow, horse, sheep, goat, pig, chicken or rooster, and sometimes a cat or dog

Play Routine

Beginning:

Have the animals greet each other by saying "hello" or "hi," or by making the appropriate animal sounds (e.g., the cow says "moo," the sheep says "baaah," or the horse says "neigh neigh"). Keep the procedure somewhat predictable, and allow the toddler to take turns modeling you. Sometimes, after the toddler imitates your actions, he will imitate your speech.

Middle:

After the animals greet one another, have them walk in and out of the barn, saying "knock knock" to open the barn's gate. Once they are in the barn, have the animals eat, go to sleep, or even go potty! Following a routine that the toddler can relate to in his life will help him to better understand the play.

End:

End the routine before the toddler loses interest. Announce that the animals are sleeping and that you should wake them up to play again later. Return toys to their proper locations.

Language Techniques:

Choices: For example, you can say, "Do you want the cow or the sheep?" or "Should the animals eat or sleep?"

Pause in anticipation: Pause three to five seconds after making a comment. Give the toddler some time to process the comment and respond. For example, you can say, "The cow is hungry" or "The cow wants to eat." Then inwardly count to five, and wait expectantly for the toddler to say something. Accept any response. If there is no response, don't push; just keep playing.

Self-talk and parallel talk: Narrate your actions and the toddler's actions. For example, "The cow is sleeping." For toddlers who are not yet talking, make snoring sounds or say one or two words such as "sleeping" while pointing to a cow that is sleeping in the barn. Improvise the type and length of the utterance based on the toddler's current language skills.

Other Tips:

Toddlers are more likely to imitate your actions and sounds if they are having fun! Remember to be animated and silly.

Bouncing Balls

Materials:

Any type of ball that is soft, such as a foam, cloth, or plastic ball that can be handled easily by a toddler

A large plastic bowl or bucket

Play Routine

Beginning:

Sit or stand in front of the toddler. Present a ball, naming it as you show it to him.

Middle:

Bounce the ball and say "bounce." Stop. Look at your toddler and then give him the ball and say "bounce" or "I'm bouncing the ball." See what he does with the ball. Next, roll the ball and say "roll" or "I'm rolling the ball." Stop. Look at your toddler and then give it to him and say "roll." Have him try to roll the ball back to you. Continue this social play routine by having the toddler squeeze or drop the ball into a large plastic bowl or bucket. Take turns with him, and set up the

End:

Have the toddler help you put the pins away. Sing a clean-up song, or tell him why he is cleaning up, for example, "Time to clean up. We're going to pick Sally up from school now," or "It's time to eat."

Language Techniques:

Self-talk and parallel talk: Narrate your actions and the toddler's actions. For example, "The pins fell down!" or "I'm rolling the ball." For toddlers who better understand when you use only one or two words, say "down" or "rolling." Improvise the type and the length of the utterance based on the toddler's current language skills.

Sentence completion tasks: While holding the ball, say "I'm holding the *ball*". Emphasize the last word. After saying it two or three times, say it again, but stop before the last word and wait for the toddler to complete the phrase: "I'm holding the _____". If the toddler needs a phonemic cue, provide the first sound of the targeted word (*b-*). Give him a few seconds to say the target word. If he doesn't say anything, complete the sentence and continue playing.

Expand: Remember, this technique should be used in moderation because you want the conversation to be natural. If the toddler says "pin down," you can say, "The pin(s) fell down!" When you are expanding, make sure to maintain the toddler's original meaning and intention as much as possible.

Other Tips:

Set the pins on a hard, flat surface. The pins tend to fall down too much if set up on a carpet.

Some sets have characters on the pins and some come in different colors. I prefer the colors and characters because they add extra layers of interest. If your pins are plain, decorate them with the toddler's favorite stickers.

This is a good movement-based activity for toddlers who are active and need to move around. However, remember to set boundaries and take turns.

Don't feel obligated to use all the pins. Depending on the toddler, you may only have to set up three or four pins.

Bubbles

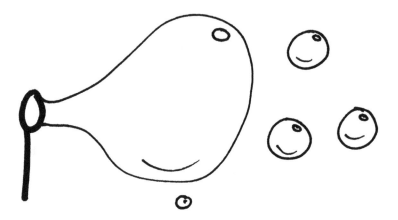

Materials:

Bubbles

Paper towels or wash cloth to dry hands

A hula hoop or a small circular round object to blow bubbles through

Play Routine

Beginning:

Open the bottle while saying something like "open" or "I'm opening the bubbles," then dip the wand into the solution while saying "dip in." Feel free to improvise what you say based on the child's understanding and ability.

Middle:

Since some toddlers have difficulty blowing bubbles, I usually start with having the toddler catch or pop bubbles. Ask him if he wants a big bubble or a small bubble. Be animated, and add lots of excitement and inflection in your voice.

Next, take turns blowing bubbles (say something like, "my turn," "your turn," or "Mary's turn", to emphasize turn taking). Encourage him to look at your lips. Try getting him to say "oo" while exhaling with force. Model this action, and see if the toddler will imitate you. Prompt him to blow onto your hand. Then have him blow already-blown bubbles that are resting on the wand. If the toddler is still struggling, that's OK! Try blowing kisses or making raspberries so he becomes more aware that his lips are involved in blowing. Rounding lips can be challenging, so don't expect it to be perfect at first. Continue blowing bubbles. Blow the bubbles up or down. Blow the bubbles to certain sections of the room and to different body parts.

End:

When I blow bubbles, my hands end up covered in bubble solution. If your hands are wet, point it out (e.g., "You have wet hands. I have wet hands too!"). For toddlers who are not talking or understanding very much, say "wet hands" while pointing to the wet hands. First, dry your own hands with the paper towel or washcloth. Next, give the paper towel or washcloth to the toddler. See if he needs help. Provide assistance if you see that he is struggling with this self-help skill.

Language Techniques:

Self-talk and parallel talk: Narrate your actions and the toddler's actions (e.g., "I'm drying my hands," "drying," or simply, "dry."). Improvise the type and the length of the utterance based on the toddler's current language skills.

Question a little, not a lot: To avoid asking too many questions, keep comments and questions to a three-to-one ratio. For instance, you can say, "There's a bubble" (first comment); "It's a big bubble" (second comment); "I'll blow another bubble" (third comment). After three comments, ask a question, such as "Want more bubbles?" For older toddlers who may understand size differences, ask, "Do you want a big bubble or a small bubble?" Accept any gesture or verbalization. If necessary, point to the bubble or say "bubble," "big bubble," or "small bubble" as a prompt if he doesn't respond after a few seconds.

Pause in anticipation: Pause three to five seconds after making a comment. Give the toddler some time to process the comment and to respond. For example, you can say, "That's a big bubble." Then count to five and wait expectantly for the toddler to say something. Accept any response. If there is no response, don't push him; just continue playing.

Other Tips:

The adult should hold the bottle of bubbles to prevent any accidents. Or use the non-spill bubbles if the toddler insists on holding the bottle.

Some bubbles come in colors, but consider yourself warned: they may stain your furniture, so blow them outside.

Chalk

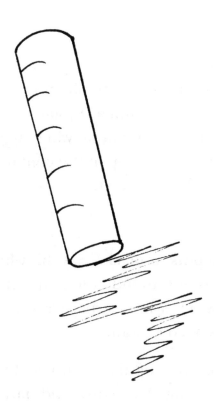

Materials:

Multicolor sidewalk chalk

A sidewalk or driveway

Play Routine

Beginning:

Start drawing! Usually, I begin by drawing huge circular motions. Watch to see what the toddler does. Present two or three pieces of chalk, and have him select a color.

Middle:

Watch the toddler draw. Narrate what he's doing using simple short utterances. Pause. Wait for him to say something. After he has finished making his creation, express your satisfaction and excitement with his work.

Next, draw something easy to identify like a sun, a house, or a face. If you draw a face, name the eyes, nose, and mouth. After you finish drawing one picture, show the toddler your drawing. Continue coloring and following a predictable routine of drawing, commenting, sharing/turn-taking, and switching chalk.

End:

Allow the toddler to finish drawing his last piece. Signify the end of the session by stating, "Time to clean up." Start singing a clean-up song. Have him help you put the chalk away. Give him a storage container, and see if he can open it independently. Set it up so that he will struggle a little with this task. Pause and wait while he attempts to open the container. Your goal here is for the toddler to indicate that help is needed.

Language Techniques:

Choices: Ask, "Do you want pink or black?" Say this while displaying the respective chalk. This question is not intended to help with color naming or color recognition (especially if he is non-verbal); rather, it's more about saying something to indicate his need or want.

Follow the toddler's lead: Copy the toddler's actions. If he starts drawing lines or circles, then do the same thing. Add words and narrate the toddler's actions in a simple yet animated way. If he points to his artwork and grunts or says something unintelligible, acknowledge his utterance by saying something about what he is pointing to (e.g., "Oh, how nice!" or "I like it.").

Gestures, pantomime, or silly sounds: If drawing a dog, make a barking sound; if drawing a cat, make a meowing sound; if drawing a cow, make a mooing sound, and so on.

Other Tips:

Draw familiar, easy-to-identify pictures and symbols.

Color with wet chalk, color on wet pavement, or after the toddler is finished, have him spray his painting with water to watch the colors run.

Dolls

Materials:

A doll

A doctor's kit

A bottle

A blanket

A brush

Adhesive bandages

Baby lotion (optional)

An empty jar of baby applesauce or a toy container of applesauce

A spoon

Keep the items in a clear plastic container.

Play Routine

Beginning:

Present the baby doll. Hold and cradle it. Sometimes I like to greet the baby using a motherese type of voice, saying for instance, "Hi baby," "Oh, what a cute baby," or "Tickle tickle baby." Feel free to say anything you like as you hold the baby. Hand the baby to the toddler. Watch what he does with it. If he is playing with the doll inappropriately, try to model the appropriate behaviors. Gently take the doll back and say, "He's a nice baby" while stroking its toes, hair, or belly. If the toddler continues to hit or throw the doll, it may be a sign that he is not yet ready for this type of play.

Middle:

After introducing the baby doll, place it on the blanket. Take the clear plastic container/kit out. Give it to the toddler and let him try to open it. Encourage him to say "help" or "open." After the container is successfully opened, introduce items in the kit by displaying and naming each one. Next, select an item or have the toddler select one. Avoid having too many items out at one time, as this can be a little distracting. Check the baby doll's ears with the otoscope, use the stethoscope to listen to the baby doll's heart (vocalize this by saying "thump thump"), take the baby doll's temperature, put lotion on the baby doll's feet, and feed it. Take your time playing with each device. It's not a race to finish playing with the items as quickly as possible.

End:

When it's approaching the end of the session, yawn and indicate that the baby doll is tired (eg., "Oh, I think the baby doll is sleepy. It's time to go night-night."). Use the same phrase that you use for the toddler's typical bedtime routine. Next, sing a bedtime song such as "Twinkle Twinkle Little Star." Lastly, put all the items back in the container, and say goodnight to the baby doll.

Language Techniques:

Self-talk and parallel talk: Periodically, narrate your actions and the toddler's actions (e.g., "I'm singing to the baby.") Improvise the type and the length of the utterance based on the toddler's current language skills.

Set it up: Take the clear plastic kit out. Give it to the toddler. See if he can open it. Wait a few seconds, and see what he does. Ask him, "Do you need help?" and then wait. Lastly, encourage the toddler to verbalize "help" or "open."

Oops!: Once the toddler is familiar with the devices, pretend to accidently feed the baby doll with a brush, or pretend that you can't find an object in plain sight. For instance, ask the toddler, "Where is the bottle? I can't find the bottle!"

Fishing for Cubes

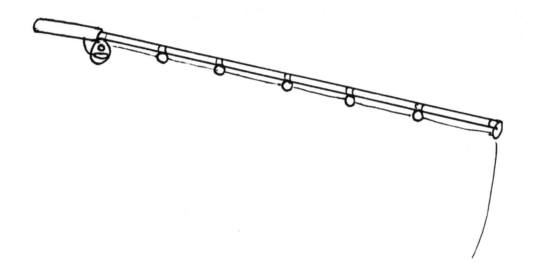

Materials:

Two buckets or large plastic mixing bowls halfway filled with water

A ladle, a fishing net, or a large spoon

Reusable plastic ice cubes (but not frozen, because you want them to float)

Towels or a washcloth

Play Routine

Beginning:

Drop the ice cubes into the water and watch them float. Look at the cubes while they float. See what the toddler does. Copy his actions. If he puts his hands in the water, put your hands in the water too.

Middle:

Pick up the ladle and fish for a cube. When you catch one, dump it into the other bucket. Give the toddler a turn to catch one or two cubes. Then take your turn again while saying, "It's my turn." Continue taking turns until all the cubes have been transferred into the other container.

End:

Dry hands with a towel or washcloth. Dump the water from the buckets into the sink while saying, "Bye-bye, water…bye-bye, water…" Give the toddler a towel or washcloth to help clean up any mess.

Language Techniques:

Self-talk and parallel talk: Periodically, narrate your actions and the toddler's actions by saying things such as "My hands are in the water," "I'm fishing," "You got a cube," or "You did it." Improvise the type and the length of the utterance based on the toddler's current language skills.

Sentence completion tasks: Use a certain phrase consistently each time you drop a cube into the water (e.g., "It goes in the water," or "Drop it in the water."). Emphasize the word *water*. Then, after saying it two or three times, say, "It goes in the _____." or "Drop it in the _____." If the toddler needs a phonemic cue, provide the first sound of the targeted word: "*w*____".Give him a few seconds to say "water," and if he doesn't say anything, you can say the word again.

Pause in anticipation: Pause three to five seconds after making a comment. Give the toddler some time to process the comment and respond. For example, you can say, "My hands are wet!" while showing your wet hands to the toddler. Then count to five and wait expectantly for the toddler to say something. Accept any response. If there is no response, just keep playing.

Other Tips:

Choose colored plastic ice cubes to add interest.

You may want to play outside or in the kitchen, just in case there are any spills.

Have the toddler wear an apron.

Touch and Explore Box

Materials:

An empty shoebox or any type of square container

Several bags of dried kidney beans and dried pasta (such as shells, farfalle, and bowtie pasta)

*** If the child is still exploring his environment by mouthing (putting objects and toys in his mouth), then it may be wise to skip this activity or use different materials to ensure safety.

Spoons, cups, whisks, and other kitchen utensils with no sharp edges

Small figurines or puzzle pieces (anything that can be hidden under the beans)

Play Routine

Beginning:

Present the box filled with the beans and pasta to the toddler. Touch the beans and encourage him to do the same. Watch and see what he does. Many toddlers enjoy touching, digging, and putting their hands under the beans. Allow your toddler time to feel this new texture and experience the sensation. Follow the toddler's lead and do the same thing that he is doing.

Middle:

Take one of the utensils and use it to move the beans and noodles. Use a spoon to pick up and then dump some beans, and while doing so, talk about what you are doing. Next, give the spoon to the toddler. Watch what he does with it. Take turns using the spoon. Teach turn taking by saying, "It's my turn…Now it's your turn," or "Now it's Jack's turn." Then introduce another utensil. Most toddlers find this activity very fun and stimulating. Once all the utensils have been used, hide puzzle pieces or other small toy objects under the beans and pasta, such as shapes from shape sorters or figurines.

End:

End the routine once all the utensils have been used and/or once the toddler has found all the objects. Sing a clean-up song and move on to a different activity.

Language Techniques:

Self-talk and parallel talk: Periodically, narrate your actions and the toddler's actions (e.g., "I'm mixing the beans" or "You're touching the beans."). Improvise the type and the length of the utterance based on the toddler's current language skills.

Pause in anticipation: Pause three to five seconds after making a comment. Give the toddler some time to process the comment and respond. For example, you can say, "I can't find the _____ (name of hidden object)," or "I don't see the _____ (name of hidden object)." Then count to five and wait expectantly for the toddler to say something. Most will try locating the hidden object. Accept any response. If there is no response, just keep playing.

Choices: You can ask the toddler what utensil he would like to use for this activity. Take out two items, and ask, for instance, "Do you want the spoon or the cup?" Say this while displaying the two items.

Little People™ Go to School

Materials:

Little People™ school bus

Several Little People™ (enough to fill the bus)

Play Routine

The following routine is quite detailed, and it involves a few more steps than the previous routines required. If your toddler is not following along or seems to get stuck on one sequence, stay with it. Just make sure you are trying to expand his words and slightly varying his play so that it's not too repetitious. Please see **Appendix D: How Play Relates to Language** to help you figure out your toddler's play level.

Beginning:

Pretend that all the Little People™ are sleeping. Lay them down and make snoring sounds. Kids LOVE this! Then wake up the figures individually by saying, "Wake up, little boy," and "Wake up, little girl." Use the same phrase each time. After two or three times, give your toddler a turn. Pause with anticipation for him to repeat the routine. If he needs a little prompting, say, "Your turn." If he is not interested, continue the routine once more. Then pause and wait again for your toddler to follow.

Middle:

Once all the Little People™ are "awake," pull out the bus and start putting them on the bus while saying, "Get on the bus" or "on the bus." Continue this routine until all the Little People™ are on the bus. Then the ride to school begins! You and your toddler can take turns pushing the school bus. I usually like to sing the popular "The Wheels on the Bus" song when I do this routine. Pretend to go over a bump, have the figures look out the windows, comment on the bus going slow and then fast, and talk about the bus going up and down a hill or around a lake, house, and so on. When it has arrived at the school, announce its arrival, and be dramatic by changing your voice: "We're here!" Wait expectantly for your toddler to make the same announcement. Then have all the Little People™ get off the bus one by one. Narrate this by saying, "Get off the bus." Then you can take them to school and create another routine of your own. For instance, you could have them sit for circle time, sing a nursery rhyme, eat a snack, and take a nap.

End:

End the routine by putting the Little People™ back on the bus to go home.

Language Techniques:

Self-talk and parallel talk: Periodically, narrate your actions and the toddler's actions (e.g., "I'm pushing the bus," or "You're looking at the bus"). Improvise the type and the length of the utterance based on the toddler's current language skills.

Follow the toddler's lead: Copy the toddler's actions. If he is pushing the bus, allow him to do so. Add words and narrate what he is doing in a simple yet animated way, such as "You're pushing the bus." Couple this with the hand gesture for *push*. If the toddler points to bus and grunts or says something unintelligible, acknowledge his utterance by saying something about what he is pointing to ("The bus?"). Try to take a turn and add another step to the sequence. For instance, push the bus, and then make it go around a chair or under a table.

Gestures, pantomime, or silly sounds: If you sing the song "Wheels on the Bus," be sure to include the hand gestures! For instance, for the phrase, "The wheels on the bus go round and round," make two fists, and make them circle each other to mimic wheels going round and round. When the people are sleeping, pretend to snore. Some late-talking toddlers may initially be more likely to imitate certain sounds than words.

Mr. Potato Head™

Materials:

Reclosable zip-top bag

Mr. Potato Head™

Play Routine

The following routine is quite detailed and involves a few extra steps. Please see **Appendix D: How Play Relates to Language** to help you figure out your toddler's play level. If this is your toddler's first time playing with a Mr. Potato Head™, I advise starting with an intact Potato Head™ and having the toddler pull each piece out. This will be a little easier and will help to familiarize him with the placement of the parts.

Beginning:

Give the head of the Mr. Potato Head™ toy to your toddler, saying, "Here's Mr. Potato Head™" slowly and dramatically. Say, "I'm taking out the shoes," while removing the shoes from the bag. I prefer to start with his shoes because they help Mr. Potato Head™ stand. Display the shoes, naming them again: "Shoes." Wait a few seconds for him to imitate the word *shoes*. Give the shoes to your toddler even if he does not imitate your utterance. Praise any attempt. Provide assistance if he needs help putting on the shoes.

Middle:

After the toy is standing, say, "Mr. Potato Head™ can walk." Say this while you walk the toy with your hands. "But, uh oh, he keeps falling down [show him falling down] because he can't see" (point to your own eyes). Display the eyes, labeling them again as *eyes*. Wait a few seconds for the toddler to imitate the word *eyes*. Give the eyes to your toddler even if he does not imitate your utterance. Praise any of his attempts.

End:

Continue this routine with the remaining items. Try to use the same phrases so that the sequence of presenting the objects is predictable. This decreases the cognitive load and helps the toddler feel somewhat in control. Once Mr. Potato Head™ has been put together, take him apart!

Language Techniques:

Sentence completion tasks: While holding the eyes, say, "He needs *eyes*." Emphasize the word *eyes*. Then, after saying it two or three times, say it again, but leave off the word *eyes* and wait for the toddler to complete the phrase: "He needs _____" . If the toddler needs a phonemic cue, provide the first sound of the targeted word. Give him a few seconds to say "eyes," and if he doesn't say anything, then say the word again and continue playing.

Oops: Once the toddler is familiar with placement of the body parts (this can take a while), purposefully put a part in the wrong place. For instance, put an arm on Potato Head™'s head or feet. See if the toddler notices the error. If he does, have him fix it.

Expand: This technique should be used in moderation because you want the conversation to be natural. If the toddler says something like, "Eat apple", you can say, "Yes, you are eating an apple" or "eating an apple". When you are expanding on your toddler's utterance, make sure to maintain the toddler's original meaning and intention as much as possible.

Other Tips:

The toddler should not be required to request each piece verbally, as this may be too demanding for his language skill level, which will take away the fun of the activity and make it stressful.

I like to link the objects to their functions. Therefore, the hands are linked to touching and waving, the nose to smelling, and the mouth to eating and talking.

Memory Time!

Materials:

Three or four miscellaneous objects (e.g., puzzle pieces, blocks, crayons, cars)

Washcloth

Play Routine

This activity is recommended for toddlers who are a little older and understand that objects can disappear and reappear. Please see **Appendix D: How Play Relates to Language** for more information.

Beginning:

Introduce each object one-by-one to your toddler. Hold up each item, saying, "I have a *cow*" (pause for three seconds, counting inwardly *one Mississippi, two Mississippi, three Mississippi*); "I have a *truck*" (pause again for three seconds); "I have a *car*" (pause for three seconds). Next, play with the items. Make the cow moo, push the truck, and have the car beep at the cow. Do anything that comes to mind. Take turns playing with each item.

Middle:

Once you feel the toddler has become familiar with the items, take out the washcloth or towel and tell the toddler it is magical. You can either tell the toddler that you are going to cover the items with the magical towel, or you can just cover them. With the three items hidden under the towel, remove one of them without the toddler seeing it. Lift up the towel and say, "Ta-dah!" Name the two remaining pieces and then ask what happened to the other piece: "Here's the _____. Here's the _____. Where's the _____?"

End:

After taking several turns, announce that the magical towel or magical wash-cloth needs a rest. Have the toddler help you put the remaining items back in place. Move on to playing with another toy, or continue with your daily routine.

Language Tips:

Question a little, not a lot: To avoid asking too many questions, keep comments and questions to a three-to-one ratio. For instance, you can say, "Here's a cow" (first comment); "Here's a truck" (second comment); "Here's a car" (third comment). Cover the items with the magical towel, and remove a piece. Follow this with a question: "What's missing?" Say this while pointing to the remaining items. Accept any gesture or verbalization that the toddler makes. Wait a few seconds and then reveal the missing item.

Pause in anticipation: Pause three to five seconds after making a comment. Give the toddler some time to process the comment and then to respond. For example, you can say, "I'm covering the puzzle pieces! Bye-bye, cow. Bye-bye, truck. Bye-bye, car." Say this while covering each piece with the towel. Then count to five and wait expectantly for the toddler to say something. Accept any response. If there is no response, don't push; it's better to stop playing.

Choices: Ask the toddler what three pieces he would like to choose for this activity. Take out a puzzle or some of his favorite figurines. "Do you want the car or the airplane?" Say this while holding up the two items.

Other Tips:

For younger toddlers, use two objects only.

To make it more challenging for older toddlers, increase the amount of objects, or introduce the concept of categories indirectly by including animals, cars, or people.

Play dough

Materials:

Two or three containers of play dough (any color, but use one color at a time)

Two or three plastic cookie cutters

One or two toy rolling pins

Pebbles

Cookie sheet

Play Routine

If this is your toddler's first time playing with play dough, give him time to explore and feel this unusual texture. Many toddlers like to poke it, tear it, rip it, and push it. Try not to force the toddler to make a shape with the play dough. Do that once he's explored this texture and has become comfortable with it.

Beginning:

Give one container to the toddler and say, "Open, please." Most likely, he will not be able to open it and will hand the container back to you. Wait expectantly for him to verbalize what he wants you to do. If he doesn't say anything, encourage him to say "help" or "open." Then open the container and narrate the action (e.g., "I'm opening the play dough" or "Open play dough"). Next, take the play dough out of the container. Flip it over, tap the bottom, and squeeze the sides, saying something like, "Tap tap, squeeze squeeze" while simultaneously doing these actions. Be careful not to let the play dough fall out, because you want to take turns and allow your toddler the opportunity to "tap tap, squeeze squeeze."

Middle:

Watch your toddler interact with the play dough. If he is playing appropriately with the play dough (i.e., making a ball or pushing it down), imitate his actions. If your toddler doesn't know what to do, show him by pushing down the play dough or rolling it with the rolling pin. If he is ready to use cookie cutters, do this step next. Give your toddler a choice of which cookie cutter he wants to use (e.g., "Do you want the dog or the cat?"). Show each cutter while asking the question. Make a snowman, make worms or snakes, make a ball, or make pretend food and serve it to your toddler's favorite stuffed animal.

End:

Once your toddler has played with the play dough for quite some time, end the task before he becomes bored with it. Always end an activity on a good note. Have him help you clean up the play dough and put it back into its container. Make it a game to find all the remaining play dough pieces.

Language Tips:

Self-talk and parallel talk: Periodically, narrate your actions and the toddler's actions (e.g., "push down," "roll out," "press the dough," or "roll the dough." Improvise the type and the length of the utterance based on the toddler's current language skills.

Set it up: Give one play dough container to the toddler. See if he can open it. Wait a few seconds, and see what he does. Ask, "Do you need help?" and then wait. Lastly, encourage the toddler to verbalize the words "help" or "open."

Follow the toddler's lead: Copy the toddler's actions. If the toddler is poking the play dough with his fingers and exploring this new texture, do the same thing! Try to understand his perspective by interacting at his level. Add words and narrate what the toddler is doing in a simple yet animated way (e.g., "You're making a ball!"). If the toddler points to the play dough and grunts or says something unintelligible, acknowledge his utterance by saying something about what he is pointing to ("the play dough?"). Then take a turn, and add another step to his play. For example, if he is continually poking the play dough, poke it with him for a little while, and then make eyes, a nose, and a mouth with the impressions. If the toddler's play is a little repetitious and one-dimensional, think about how you can expand it to add another level of complexity.

Other Tips:

I highly recommend playing with play dough on a large cookie sheet or tarp sheet so that you don't end up with a big mess. A cookie tray will provide a smooth nonstick surface to work on and help to contain all the sticky bits.

Puppets

Materials:

One or two puppets that have open, moveable mouths

Plastic food (optional for older/more mature toddlers)

Play Routine

Beginning:

I like to introduce the puppet by putting it on my hand without the toddler seeing me do so. Give it some personality. You want the toddler to be entertained and engaged, not scared, so make the puppet shy or goofy. Slowly have it peak out of a corner or up from behind the couch. Have a puppet version of peek-a-boo, but continue to have the puppet jump in and out a few times. Most toddlers enjoy this interaction!

Middle:

For toddlers who are not talking yet, model sounds or one-syllable words such as *ah, oo, yay,* and *hi.* Have the puppet look into the toddler's mouth, and ask him to say "ah." Have the puppet blow kisses, hug the toddler, sit next to him, or trip and fall down. Pretend to feed the puppet some plastic toy food. You can say, "I'm so hungry" as though you are speaking for the puppet.

End:

To wrap things up, announce that the puppet is tired and needs to take a nap. Sing the puppet a song, and then say "night night." Put the toy items back where they belong.

Language Techniques:

Oops: Make the puppet walk, skip, and jump but then accidently trip. Narrate this by saying, for instance, "Oops, I fell down!" or "Fell down!" Look at the toddler and assess his reaction. Help the puppet up and ask the puppet, "Are you OK?"

Expand: This technique should be used in moderation because you want the conversation to be natural. If the toddler says something such as "puppet talk," then you can say, "Yes, the puppet is talking." When you are expanding, make sure to maintain the toddler's original meaning and intention as much as possible.

Gestures, pantomime, or silly sounds: Some late-talking toddlers may initially be more likely to imitate certain sounds than words, so be animated by making the puppet open his mouth very widely to say "ah" or "ah hah!" Have two puppets greet each other by saying "hi" and "hello," or have the puppet sing simple songs containing only single syllables such as "doh, ray, me, fah, so, lah, ti, doh" or "ee, eye, ee, eye, oh."

Puzzles

Materials:

Any peg or chunky puzzle

Any puzzle that is related to a category (e.g., farm, transportation, or ocean)

Play Routine

Beginning:

Remove the puzzle pieces from the puzzle. I keep my puzzle pieces in a clear plastic bag. Present one or two puzzle pieces at a time, and ask the toddler which one he wants. Accept gestures or pointing. Allow him the chance to put the piece in the correct space. If he is struggling, provide assistance.

Middle:

Continue completing the puzzle. Try to make the sounds for each animal or vehicle. If it's an animal puzzle, I may also pet each animal or pretend to give it something to eat. For the older toddler, talk about where the animals live, their size (e.g., "A cow is big" and "A bunny is small") or what they eat (e.g., "Dogs eat bones" and "Bunnies eat carrots").

End:

When it's time to clean up, help the toddler remove the puzzle pieces by playing an easy, fun identification game with him. Say, for instance, "Where is the chicken?" or "I see a horse. Do you see it?" Pretend you can't find a piece (e.g., "Hmm...where is the fire truck?"). Do this for each piece until all the pieces are in the bag.

Language Techniques:

Sentence completion tasks: While holding a certain puzzle piece, say what it is. For example, "I have a *pig*." Feel free to say any short and simple phrase. Just make sure the final word is the target word. Emphasize the word *pig*. Then, after saying it two or three times, say it again, but stop before the word pig and allow the toddler to complete the phrase: "I have a _____" If the toddler needs a phonemic cue, provide the first sound of the targeted word: "I have a *p*...." Give him a few seconds to say "pig," and if he doesn't say anything, say the word again and continue playing.

Oops: Once the toddler becomes familiar with the puzzle, I like to put the pieces in the wrong hole so I can ask the toddler to help me, or I can target words he might say in response to my mistake, such as "no," "not there," or "uh-uh."

Choices: Ask the toddler if he would prefer the animal puzzle or the truck puzzle. Once he has made a decision, ask him periodically which puzzle piece he'd like to put in next. For instance, "Do you want the sheep or the pig?" Encourage verbal responses by saying, "Now you try: say *pig*."

Other Tips:

With younger toddlers, it is best to start with a completed puzzle. This way your toddler will have a frame of reference as to where the pieces go. Then he can remove the pieces one by one and put them back in.

Puzzles that have a matching picture of the design in the tray of the puzzle (underneath the pieces) also help to visually guide the toddler to identify the correct spot for each piece.

If your toddler is having difficulty or becoming frustrated, use puzzles with fewer pieces or pieces that are bigger in size with simpler designs and with pegs.

I have found that when a toddler is struggling with acquiring language, it is best not to focus on teaching shapes, numbers, and the alphabet. This is because these concepts aren't yet functional for the toddler. Learning these words will not help your toddler to communicate his needs and wants on a daily basis. It's best to focus on words that are relevant to his daily routine.

Scarves

Materials

Five to ten different-colored scarves or rags knotted or sewed together to make one long scarf

A coffee can with a flexible lid

> Cut a hole in the lid and push the scarves all the way to the bottom of the can so that the scarves or rags are not exposed.

Play Routine

Beginning:

Show the coffee can to the toddler. Shake the can and say, "Shake shake shake," and then hold it upside down. Hand the coffee can to the toddler. See what he does with it. He might imitate your actions or investigate the can.

Middle:

Watch the toddler as he explores the coffee can. Narrate his actions, and describe what he's looking at or what he sees. If the toddler does not attempt to remove the scarves with his hands, ask to have the can back by saying, "Can, please," or "I want the can, please." Next, insert your hand through the hole and pull the scarf so that just the tip is exposed through the hole. When it shows, announce it by saying, "Tah dah!" Pause and look at the toddler expectantly. What do you think he's thinking? Hand the can back to the toddler. Most will pull out the scarves. If he doesn't, model what to do, then hand the can to him and encourage him to try. Once you've pulled out the scarves, indicate that the can is empty, or that there are no more scarves, by saying, "No more." Perform the routine again, but remove the scarves very slowly. Exaggerate your movements. Then remove the scarves very quickly. Once again, exaggerate your movements.

End:

End the play after a few turns or right before you sense the toddler has had enough. Say bye-bye to the scarves or sing a clean-up song.

Language Techniques:

Self-talk and parallel talk: Periodically, narrate your actions and the toddler's actions ("Pull out," "I'm shaking the tin," or "I'm pulling out the scarf."). Improvise the type and the length of the utterance based on the toddler's current language skills.

Set it up: Put the lid on the can and give it to the toddler. Wait a few seconds and see if he opens it. If he seems unable to open it, say, "Do you need help?" and then wait a bit more. Lastly, encourage the toddler to say "help" or "open."

Pause in anticipation: Pause three to five seconds after making a comment. Give the toddler some time to process the comment and then to respond. For example, you can say, "This scarf is so soft." Say this while touching the scarf. Then count to five and wait expectantly for the toddler to say something. Accept any response. If there is no response, just keep playing.

Other Tips:

For older toddlers, use scarves with designs so he can describe the differences.

Scavenger Hunt

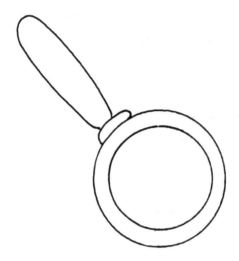

Materials:

One or two miscellaneous items (hide only one at a time)

Play Routine

Beginning:

Until the toddler gets the hang of it, hide only one item at a time. Display and name the item. Next, tell the toddler that you are going to hide the item. Tell him not to look, and cover your eyes while saying, "No peeking" or "No looking." Then hide the item, narrating your action: "I'm hiding the _____." For younger toddlers, don't hide the item under a blanket. Hide the item in the open so that he can easily find it. For instance, place it on the couch so that he can see it and understand the concept of the game.

Middle:

Have the toddler find the item. Repeat the same phrase: "Where is the _____ (name of item)?" or "I'm looking for the _____." If the toddler is not imitating your words, that's OK. Incorporate dramatic actions, such as putting your hand to your forehead while you are looking. Toddlers LOVE acting out, especially if an adult is doing it too! When the toddler finds the object, make a big commotion by exclaiming, "You found it!" followed by clapping. Once the toddler has found the object a few times, recruit an older sibling, a playmate, or your partner, and have the toddler hide the item this time. Point out a few places for the toddler to hide the object. Continue the routine.

End:

Once the toddler has tried to find the item a few times, announce that it is time to do something else, such as take a nap, eat lunch, or pick up Johnny from school. Have the toddler help you put the items away.

Language Techniques:

Question a little, not a lot: To avoid asking too many questions, keep comments and questions to a three-to-one ratio. For instance, you can say, "Hmm…I'm looking for the cow" (first comment); "I'll look under the couch" (second comment); "Now I'll look under the table" (third comment). Then you can ask, "Where is the cow hiding?" Say this while putting your hands up with palms upward. Accept any gesture or verbalization. Wait for the toddler to show you where the hidden item is located.

Expand: This technique should be used in moderation because you want the conversation to be natural. If the toddler says "cow hide," then you can say, "The cow is hiding." When you are expanding, make sure to maintain the toddler's original meaning and intention as much as possible.

Gestures, pantomime, or silly sounds: Some late-talking toddlers may initially be more likely to imitate certain sounds than words, so be animated during the scavenger hunt by putting your hand to your forehead while you are looking. Scratch your head and squint your eyes as though you are thinking very hard about this predicament. Ask where it is hiding by putting your hands up and palms upward, and become very excited when you find the "hidden" piece.

Other Tips:

To make the scavenger hunt even more fun, incorporate a flashlight, and have the toddler use the flashlight to find the item. Or have him wear a special hat when looking for the item.

Spinning Tops

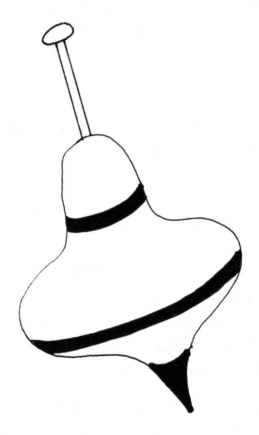

Materials:

A few different spinning tops

Play Routine

Beginning:

Show one top to the toddler and explain, "This is a top," or just say "top." Show the toddler how the top looks different from the bottom, and remark how the bottom is pointy. Next, spin the top and say, "It's spinning," or simply "spinning." Watch it spin and observe the toddler. What is he doing? Describe the top's speed ("It's going fast" or "fast") and how it slows down ("It's slowing down" or "slow"). When it comes to a stop, comment that it has stopped by saying, "It stopped!" Sometimes I like to manually stop the top, too, and I describe that action by saying "stop top." Let him try to spin a top.

Middle:

Take out another top. Have two tops spin at a time. Continue the routine above. Then introduce a third and maybe even a fourth top! Watch the tops spin and say, "Wow, the tops are spinning!"

End:

After the toddler has had enough of spinning tops, announce that it is time to move on to another activity. Close out this activity by singing the "Bye-Bye Song" from **Appendix C: Songs to End a Routine**. Have the toddler help you put the tops back in their respective places.

Language Techniques:

Sentence completion tasks: While spinning one top, say, "The top is *spinning*" or "The top is *fast.*" Or say any appropriate statement that comes to mind. Emphasize the last word. Then, after saying it two or three times, say it again, but stop before you get to the word *spinning* or *fast*, and have the toddler complete the phrase: "The top is _____." If the toddler needs a phonemic cue, provide the first sound of the targeted word (*sp-*) or (*f-*). Give him a few seconds to say the target word, and if he doesn't say anything, then say the word again and continue playing.

Oops!: Once the toddler is familiar with how to play with tops, spin the top on a carpet or rug. Of course, this will not work, but you want to see if the toddler notices why it won't spin. If he does, laugh together and have him fix the situation. If the toddler does not notice anything wrong with why the top won't spin, that's OK. Just put the top on a hard, flat surface and say, "Oops, I was being silly! It can't spin on the rug!"

Follow the toddler's lead: Copy the toddler's actions. If the toddler is looking at the tippy point of the top and exploring this new toy, then do the same thing! Try to understand his perspective by interacting at his level. Add words and narrate what the toddler is doing or possibly thinking in a simple yet animated way (e.g., "The top is pointy"). If the toddler points to the top and grunts or says something unintelligible, acknowledge his utterance by saying something about the object to which he is pointing.

Other Tips:

For older toddlers, find tops with different designs, as this gives you the opportunity to describe and talk about them.

Trains

Materials:

About eight to ten interlocking train tracks

Three or four trains—including a dumper

Two destinations:

> One to have at the beginning of the track
>
> Another to have at the end of the track
>
> Examples of destinations include a train station, farm, school, and a water tower.

Paper

Play Routine

Beginning:

Take turns putting the train tracks together. After the tracks are complete, introduce one train at a time. Push the trains around the track a few times, saying "chugga chugga chugga chugga, choo choo." Imitate the actions of your toddler and add words to what he is doing.

Middle:

If your toddler's play is repetitive and simple, add to it. Make the trains go fast, go slow, and then stop abruptly in the middle of the track. When you do this, say "stop!" followed by "go," and then have the train continue moving. Let the train go "up" and "down" the bridge and through a tunnel, then at some point let it fall off the track ("Oops!"). Since train play can become somewhat boring or monotonous, I like to add destinations. For instance, have the train start at a train station and travel to a farm, a school, a zoo, or a water tower. Load pretend rocks into the dumper train by crumbling up pieces of paper. Load these rocks one by one into the dumper. Before adding more rocks, ask your toddler if he would like more rocks.

End:

When it's time to end the play, have the trains go back to their "stations" or "home." Announce that it is time to clean up. Sing a clean-up song found in **Appendix C: Songs to End a Routine** and put the toys away. Cleaning up is part of the play routine, so make it fun and engaging. Have a race to put the items away quickly, or make it a game by giving the toddler simple directions to follow, such as "Put the blue train in the bottom bucket."

Language Techniques:

Self-talk and parallel talk: Periodically, narrate your actions and the toddler's actions ("The train is going fast," "I'm pushing the train."). Improvise the type and the length of the utterance based on the toddler's current language skills.

Pause in anticipation: Pause three to five seconds after making a comment. Give the toddler some time to process the comment and then to respond. For example, you can say, "Oops, the train fell off (the track)" or "The train needs some gas. It stopped." Then count to five and wait expectantly for the toddler to say something. Accept any response. If there is no response, don't push for one; just keep playing.

Choices: Ask the toddler if he wants the train to go "up or down." If you're making paper rocks, ask the toddler if he wants "big rocks" or "small rocks." Encourage verbal responses by saying "You try; say _____" (include the target word).

Window Cling Pictures

Materials:

Window cling pictures

Play Routine

What's so great about window clings is that they are cheap, easy to remove, readily available (can be purchased at most drug stores or online), and usually on hand for each season and holiday, and of course, toddlers LOVE them.

Beginning:

Introduce the window clings by naming them. Peel off one window cling at a time, then put it on the window. While doing so, narrate your actions. Emphasize and stress the name of the object that is being placed on the window. For instance, if putting on a cling of a dog, say, "I'm putting the *dog* on the window." Repeat the same phrase for each picture so that your toddler can become familiar with it. If you find that he is not imitating you, then say, "I'm putting the _____" while in the process of putting the cling on the window. Pause expectantly for a response to see if he finishes the sentence. If he does not, just repeat the sentence and fill in the target word.

Middle:

Next, present *two* window clings to the toddler at a time. Give him a choice: "Do you want the dog or the cat?" Then after a few turns, ask him another question: "Do you want it here or here?" Make sure to point to each location while you ask this. Or you can ask, "Do you want it at the top of the window or at the bottom of the window?" Hold the cling at the top and at the bottom of the window as you say each portion of the sentence. Asking the toddler questions encourages turn taking and lets him know that you value his input.

End:

Once all the window clings are brilliantly hanging on the windows, admire them. Then either remove them or leave them up for others to admire.

Language Techniques:

Sentence completion tasks: While you're peeling the window clings, you can say, "I'm peeling off the *dog*," thereby labeling what you are removing. Or you can say any appropriate statement that comes to mind. Emphasize the last word. Then, after saying it two or three times, say it again, but stop just before the last word and wait for the toddler to complete the phrase: "I'm peeling off the _____" If the toddler needs a phonemic cue, provide the first sound of the targeted word (*d-*). Give him a few seconds to say the target word. If he doesn't say anything, say the word again and continue playing.

Expand: This technique should be used in moderation because you want the conversation to be natural. If the toddler says "dog on," then you can say, "The dog is on the window." When you are expanding, make sure to maintain the toddler's original meaning and intention as much as possible.

Set it up: Give one window cling to the toddler. See if he can put it on the window. Some toddlers can do this without assistance. Wait a few seconds, and see what he does. If he hesitates, ask, "Do you need help?" and then wait for him to respond. Lastly, encourage the toddler to verbalize "help" or "open."

Other Tips:

Clean your windows before doing this activity to ensure that the window clings stay and do not fall off.

Arts and Crafts Activities

Coloring with Bingo Markers

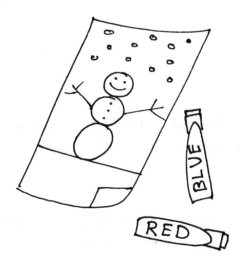

Materials:

Washable bingo markers

Plain paper or coloring books

Play Routine

Beginning:

Show the toddler two or three bingo markers. Give him one unopened marker. If the toddler struggles to open it, such as pulling the marker instead of twisting it, show him how to open the marker. Make some dots on the plain paper, and name them by saying "dot". Give the marker back to the toddler. Allow the toddler to color or make dots or do whatever he wishes.

Middle:

Take turns making dots on the paper using different colors. Once the toddler has explored using the bingo markers, take out some coloring books. Show the toddler two different pages, and ask him which one he would like to color. Wait expectantly for him to say something. Accept any pointing or gesture, and give him encouragement and praise by nodding your head while naming the picture chosen. For example, if you presented a page of Mickey Mouse and another one of Donald Duck and he pointed to Mickey Mouse, then say with a big smile, "Mickey Mouse? Do you want Mickey Mouse? Here's Mickey Mouse." Notice how in this response you are acknowledging the toddler's choice by naming the item and repeating the item's name a few times. Multiple repetitions help the toddler acquire new language. Color the pictures. Don't worry how well he colors the pictures. Praise the process, not the result!

End:

End this task once you've completed coloring a few pages or right before you feel the toddler has lost interest.

Language Techniques:

Self-talk and parallel talk: Periodically, narrate your actions and the toddler's actions. For example, say "twist" or "twist off" while showing the toddler how you are twisting off the cap. Demonstrate the actions in a purposeful manner, and carefully select words that appropriately describe your actions. Improvise the type and the length of the utterance based on the toddler's current language skills.

Choices: Show or point to two different objects, and ask the toddler for his preference. In this case, "Do you want red or blue?" or "Do you want to color the dog or the cat?" Encourage verbal responses by saying, "Now you try; say_____" (*red, dog, cat*, or whatever the target word is).

Set it up: Give the toddler an unopened bingo marker, and see if he can open it. Some toddlers can do this without assistance. Wait a few seconds to see what he does. If he hesitates, ask, "Do you need help?" and then wait. Lastly, encourage the toddler to verbalize "help" or "open."

Other Tips:

Try to control the number of bingo markers in use so that the toddler has to ask you for an additional one. For a toddler who prefers to use the same color (some do!), encourage him to vary the routine by asking if he would like a different marker.

Drying the Clothes

Materials

Rope

Wooden Clothespins with a rounded head and two legs

*** Avoid using the clothespins with the hinges that need to be squeezed, because you don't want pinched fingers.

Toddler's clothing:

> Socks, underwear, pants, t-shirts, sweaters (limit to five or six items)

Two chairs

Pictures

Play Routine

This activity is recommended for toddlers who can follow multistep commands.

Beginning:

Present the rope and clothespins in a clear reclosable zip-top bag. Remove the rope from the bag and name it "rope." Let your toddler see and touch it, but do not let him hold it. Tie one end of the rope to a chair while saying, "I'm tying the rope to the chair." Do this to the other end, too.

Middle:

Take one article of clothing and name it (for instance, "socks"). As you place one sock on the clothesline, say, "I'm putting the sock on the rope" or "on the rope" or "sock on." Present the clothespin to your toddler and say, "Here's the pin." Give the pin to the toddler, and see if he can secure the sock to the clothesline. He will most likely need your help. Try not to help until he communicates this to you. At this point, toddlers are usually VERY eager to put another article of clothing on the clothesline. So present a sock, naming it "sock." However, do not give it to him right away. While you say "sock," dangle it and hold it close to you. Wait expectantly for him to say "sock" (count to five), and then say "sock" again and give him the sock. If he imitates you, encourage him to say "sock please." Watch as he places the sock on the clothesline. Next, your toddler will want to take the clothespin. Present the pin, labeling it "pin," but remember not to give it to him right away. Hold it, wait expectantly, and then say "pin" again. Praise any attempts he makes to repeat the word by immediately giving him the clothespin. Continue this until all the clothes are on the line.

End:

Have the toddler follow directions to help remove the clothes from the line. You can say, "Give me the socks," "Give me the t-shirt," or "Johnny, give me the sweater." I like to sing a song when completing this activity: please see **Appendix C: Songs to End a Routine** to select a song.

Language Techniques:

Pause in anticipation: Pause three to five seconds after making a comment. Give the toddler some time to process the comment and then to respond. For example, you can present a shirt, naming it "shirt." However, do not give it to him right away. While you say "shirt," hold it out in front of the toddler. Wait for him to say "shirt" (count to three or five), and then say "shirt" again and give it to him.

Question a little, not a lot: To avoid asking too many questions, keep comments and questions to a three-to-one ratio. For instance, you can say, "The socks are on the rope" (first comment); "Let's put another item on the rope" (second comment); "Hmm...I see a shirt and a sweater" (third comment). After three comments, you can ask, "What should we hang next?" Say this while putting your hands up with palms upward. Accept any gesture or verbalization from the toddler. Wait for the toddler to make a decision.

Gestures, pantomime, or silly sounds: Some late-talking toddlers may initially be more likely to imitate certain sounds than words, so be animated by pretending the socks are smelly; hold your nose and say, "Peeu! Stinky socks!" Toddlers usually think this is funny and copy your actions, attempting to say "peeu" or "stinky."

Felt Stickers

Materials:

Felt stickers—preferably ones related to a theme, such as animals, sports, or superheroes

Paper

Play Routine

Beginning:

Draw a picture of a house, a barn, or a boat—anything you want. Think about drawing something that will allow you to incorporate the theme of the stickers. Ask the toddler what should be drawn: "Should I draw a house or should I draw a car?" Let the toddler be involved in the decision making. Talk about what you are drawing by saying, "I'm drawing a house."

Middle:

After you finish drawing your picture, show the toddler some stickers. Incorporate stickers that will complement your picture. For instance, if you draw a house, use stickers that apply to the house, such as animals, flowers, bugs, and people. Peel off one sticker, naming it as you do so. Next, think aloud about where it should go. Ask the toddler, "Should I put the _____ here or here?" Give the toddler a chance to answer the question. Inwardly count to five using the one- Mississippi, two-Mississippi, three-Mississippi (and so on) method. Accept any gesture, sound, or utterance from the toddler as a turn in the conversation. Shape his utterance into a word to represent his intention. For instance, if he says "hou" while pointing to the house, then say "house." This way the toddler knows that you are responding to his utterance. Continue decorating the paper with stickers to create a scene.

End:

When you have exhausted your stickers, say "tah-dah" or "It's finished!" Display the picture where all can admire it.

Language Techniques:

Sentence completion tasks: While drawing your picture, say what you are drawing: "I'm drawing a *house*." Emphasize the last word. After saying it two or three times, say it again, but stop before the last word and wait for the toddler to complete the phrase(e.g.,"I'm drawing a _____"). If the toddler needs a phonemic cue, provide the first sound of the targeted word (*h*-). Give him a few seconds to say the target word. If he doesn't say anything, complete the sentence and continue playing.

Expand: This technique should be used in moderation because you want the conversation to be natural. If the toddler says "cat grass," then you can say, "The cat is on the grass." When you are expanding, make sure to maintain the toddler's original meaning and intention as much as possible.

Choices: If using animal stickers, ask the toddler what animal he wants: "Do you want the dog or the cat?" Ask the toddler where he wants the animal placed. Encourage verbal responses by saying, "You try; say _____" (include the target word).

Other Tips:

Toddlers love felt stickers, foam stickers, glittery stickers—anything that's colorful with different textures.

Homemade Gift Bags

Materials:

Used paper shopping bags with handles

Pictures of favorite characters and familiar objects cut from magazines or printed from the Internet and family members (five to seven should be sufficient)

Two glue sticks

Play Routine

Beginning:

Lay each picture flat on a surface. Describe some of the features of each picture. For instance, if it's a photo, talk about the event or action (e.g., "Mom is swimming," "Bobby's birthday party," or "It's a pretty flower."). Take turns with the toddler, and allow him to say something about the pictures. Once you've introduced some of the pictures, start gluing!

Middle:

Give your toddler an unopened glue stick. Watch what he does. If he cannot open it, wait expectantly for him to say "help" or "open." If he hands it back to you, encourage him to say "help" or "open." Wait five seconds with an expectant look, tempting him to imitate "help" or "open." Some toddlers need help gluing, especially on the proper side of the picture. Place the pictures all over the bag.

End:

After all the pictures have been glued, make a big fuss about the awesome gift bag. Make an announcement that signals completion of the activity, such as "We're all done!" Set the bag aside. Have the toddler help you clean up, and then move on to something else.

Language Techniques:

Set it up: Give the glue stick to the toddler. See if he can open it. Some toddlers can do this without assistance. Wait a few seconds and see what he does. Say, "Do you need help?" "Help?" or "Open?" Wait. Encourage the toddler to verbalize "help" or "open."

Oops: If your toddler demonstrates stronger comprehension skills, incorrectly name a picture. For instance, if the picture is of a dog, say, "Here's the cat." See if he notices the error. If he does, you will most likely be corrected ("No!"). However, I would advise that you only make these errors once you know the toddler adequately understands a specific word, concept, or routine.

Follow the toddler's lead: Mimic the toddler's actions. If he is looking at all the pictures, give him time to look at them carefully. Try to understand his perspective by interacting with him at his level. Add words and narrate in a simple, animated way what the toddler is seeing or doing. If he points to a picture and grunts or says something unintelligible, acknowledge his utterance by saying something about what he is pointing to.

Other Tips:

I highly recommend that you make an effort to use the bag you have decorated with your toddler. Doing so will make your toddler feel proud, and it may give him an opportunity to talk about his creation!

Painting in a Box

Materials:

Shoebox

Washable finger paint (different colors)

Ping-pong balls (two or three)

Paper—preferably construction paper or thick/sturdy white paper that can fit inside your shoebox

Tape

Large cookie tray or an old towel

Play Routine

Beginning:

Put paper in the shoebox. Tape down the sides of the paper ("Let's tape the paper."). Squeeze paint onto the paper. Ask the toddler to choose colors, for instance, "Do you want red or blue?" Then ask if he wants to help squeeze the paint: "Would you like to help me paint?" Watch out—this could be the messiest part of the project, so if your toddler is squeezing the paint, make sure you at least have your hand on the paint bottle too. After squeezing out several spots of paint (about a dime or a quarter size), drop one ball in at a time. Once all the balls are in the box, put on the lid.

Middle:

Next, move the box sideways so that the balls roll back and forth. After rolling the balls in the box, shake the box. Make sure the lid is on tight.

End:

After rolling and shaking, open the box to reveal the toddler's piece of art. Talk about the colors and the designs. Next, remove the now-painted piece of paper from the box and let it dry!

Language Techniques:

Pause in anticipation: Pause three to five seconds after making a comment. Give the toddler some time to process the comment and then to respond. For example, you can say, "Here's the blue paint," "Squeeze the blue paint," or "This is so pretty" (when admiring the finished picture). Then inwardly count to five and wait expectantly for the toddler to respond. Accept any response. If there is no response, don't push for one; just keep playing.

Self-talk and parallel talk: Periodically, narrate your actions and the toddler's actions (e.g.,"I'm squeezing the bottle," "Shake it!" or "I'm shaking the box."). Improvise the type and the length of the utterance based on the toddler's current language skills.

Gestures, pantomime, or silly sounds: Some late-talking toddlers may be more likely to imitate certain sounds rather than words, so be animated during the activity by shaking your hands to demonstrate shaking the box, or pretend to squeeze something with your hand when saying "squeeze."

Painting with Markers

Materials:

Paper plates

Spray water bottle (fill bottle about a ¼ full)

Water-based nontoxic washable markers (put in a reclosable zip-top bag)

Cookie tray (to put under paper plate)

Play Routine

Beginning:

Present items one by one in an enthusiastic manner. Slowly name each item. Place the items within your toddler's sight but out of his reach. This is because you want them to verbally request each desired item. Give yourself a paper plate ("Here's my plate!"), but don't give one to the toddler. See how he responds. He'll probably want a plate too! Wait expectantly for him to say or indicate something. Immediately reward and praise any verbal attempt. When you're giving him a plate, say what you're doing ("Here's your plate, Johnny") Repetitions paired with visual cues are very important.

Middle:

Give the toddler the reclosable zip-top bag filled with washable markers. Let him try to open the bag without any assistance. If he is having difficulty, encourage him to say "help" or "open." Once the bag is open, take out two markers and give him a choice ("Do you want the green marker or the blue marker?"). Once again, wait expectantly, then repeat the words. Praise any verbal attempts. Once the toddler has a marker, he can start coloring the paper plate. Join him and color too. Talk about what you're coloring using simple but grammatically correct speech: "I'm coloring the plate" or "I'm drawing a star." Continue this until the plate is very colorful. Then the really fun part begins! Have your toddler spray the plate with water and watch the colors run. All toddlers LOVE this!

End:

Set the paper plate aside to dry, and have the toddler help you clean up by singing a clean-up song.

Language Techniques:

Set it up: Give the toddler the plastic bag. See if he can open the bag without any assistance. Wait a few seconds and see what he does. Say, "Do you need help?" Wait for a response. Lastly, encourage the toddler to verbalize "help" or "open."

Question a little, not a lot: To avoid asking too many questions, keep comments and questions to a three-to-one ratio. For instance, you can say, "I like your picture" (first comment); "That's a pretty picture" (second comment); "I'm drawing a _____" (name what you are drawing) (third comment). Then ask a question: "Are you drawing a _____?" Say this while pointing to the toddler's picture. Accept any gesture or verbalization.

Expand: This technique should be used in moderation because you want the conversation to be natural. If the toddler says "plate wet," for example, you can say, "The plate is wet. We will let it dry."

Appendices

Appendix A

Track Your Toddler's Vocabulary Growth

Directions:

Pick a time when you can spend five to fifteen minutes tracking your toddler's verbalizations. This can be at a set time of the day or whenever you're following a typical routine—such as during breakfast, while helping your toddler get dressed, or while helping him take a bath. This can also be done during a play activity. Set a goal to keep track of your toddler's word growth and verbalizations regularly, such as once a week or once every other week. This will help you track his progress. During this time, consciously write down any communicative attempts or words that he produces. Record them on the chart below.

For toddlers who have reached the fifty-word benchmark, try tracking particular parts of speech (nouns, verbs, and adjectives) and types of word combinations (noun + verb or noun + adjective). This may help you determine any areas of weaknesses, which can help guide your efforts. Try tracking his word productions once a week for a few months in order to monitor his progress.

> ❖ _My Toddler Talks: Word Tracker_ **is also available in the iTunes Store! This straightforward and easy to use app will make tracking your toddler's speech a cinch!**

Child's Name: _____

Age: _____

Date: _____

Activity/Routine:_____

Note: An utterance is any spoken sound, word, or phrase. It does not have to be intelligible.

Child's Utterance	Target Word(s) or Phrase(s)	Number of Words (per Utterance)	OPTIONAL Part of Speech or Type of Word Combination (Noun, Verb, Adjective)

Example:

Child's Name: Johnny Smith

Age: 26 months

Date: X/X/XX

Activity: Ball Play

Child's Utterance	Target Word	Number of Words (per Utterance)	Part of Speech or Type of Word Combination (Noun, Verb, Adjective)
"Ba"	Ball	1	Noun
"Da big ba"	The big ball	3	Article Adjective, Noun
"My mama"	My mama	2	Possessive (my), Noun

Appendix B

Making Routines for Your Toddler

Brainstorm:

Think about all your chores and what you need to do during a given day or week. Then ponder your child's needs: sleep, play, potty, food, stimulation, and so on. Is he involved in any special activities or classes on a weekly basis? Record everything on the chart, or make a separate list.

Must-Dos (Parents)	Frequency	Must-Dos (Child)	Frequency	Activities/ Events	Frequency

Outline:

Plan morning, afternoon, and evening routines based on the must-dos and additional special activities. Allow for flexibility and spontaneity, and try not to be overly fixated on a certain time or duration. Be more mindful about the sequence of events and transitions that take place between events and scheduled activities.

Here's an example of some things you may include (please modify as needed):

Morning	Afternoon	Evening
Wake up	Lunch	Other
Change diaper/toilet train/brush teeth	Prep for nap (read a book, rub his back, sing or listen to some lullabies)	More chores
Get dressed		More play
Eat breakfast	Nap	Prep for dinner (optional: try to involve the child)
Free play	Snack after nap	Dinner
Play time with adult	Play some more	Play
Other	Run errands	Wind down
	Other	Bath
		Put on pajamas
		Read a book
		Lights out!

Apply:

Implement the schedule.

Revise:

Adapt the routine as necessary to foster optimal learning. Are there certain routines or events that your toddler doesn't like? Do find that he is better at a particular time in the day? For instance, is he more focused and attentive after his nap or very early in the morning? Find the time that works best for you and your toddler.

Appendix C

Songs to End a Routine

"The Clean-Up Song"

Tune: Ask any preschool teacher to sing this song for you. It's very common in the preschool circuit.

Clean up, clean up
Everybody get some toys.
Clean up, clean up
All the little girls and boys.
Clean up, clean up
Everybody do your share.
Clean up, clean up
Everybody, everywhere.

"Let's Clean Up"

I learned this song from a parent a
few years ago and have been using it ever since!

Tune: "Farmer in the Dell"

Let's clean up today
Let's clean up today
We've had our fun
Our day is done.
So let's clean up today.

"Bye-Bye Song"

Tune: Improvise

Bye-bye, _____ (name of object), bye-bye, _____ (name of object)
I'll see you on _____ (name a day of the week) or
I'll see you the next time.

Appendix D

How Play Relates to Language

Many years ago, a very insightful speech-language pathologist named Carol Westby developed a play scale to help speech pathologists appropriately target language structures in language-delayed children. She found that it was necessary to assess a child's language skills based on their symbolic play skills. This is because before a child can speak, he must possess specific cognitive prerequisites for learning particular linguistic concepts. For instance, for a child to understand that blocks can be constructed to represent a house, he must understand that words are not objects but are symbols or representation of the object. For our purposes, I have summarized eight of the ten stages of play to increase awareness and understanding of how certain play skills must be in place before certain linguistic concepts can be learned.

Stage 1: Nine to twelve months old

Develops *object permanence*. This means that the child will continue to look for a hidden object that he can no longer see, hear, or touch. This is because he now understands that an object continues to exist even if it is out of sight.

Displays *means-end abilities*. The child will intentionally perform an action or a series of actions to achieve a result. For instance, he will walk to a desired object or pull a string to get it.

Will not immediately mouth (i.e. put toys in his mouth) or bang all toys but rather, will start to play with a few toys appropriately.

How does this relate to the language of a nine-to-twelve-month-old child?

The child uses words as labels because they are only produced when performing a certain activity and not uttered during other contexts. Therefore, the young child's first words are context-bound because he doesn't yet fully understand that the same word can represent meaning in a different situation or context. For instance, this child will say "car" when playing with a certain car, but he will not say it when sitting in a car.

Stage 2: Thirteen to seventeen months old

Explores toys and tries to figure out how the toys work by pushing, pulling, turning, shaking, or pounding parts to produce a reaction.

Will hand the toy to an adult if he cannot figure it out. When this happens, the child understands that adults can make changes to objects.

How does this relate to the language of a thirteen-to-seventeen-month-old child?

Single words continue to be very dependent on the context. However, verbal communication is becoming more intentional and consistent.

Stage 3: Seventeen to nineteen months old

Participates in *autosymbolic play*, which means that the symbolic play is performed with the child's own body. The child playfully pretends to sleep, eat from a spoon, or drink from a cup. At this stage, for instance, if the child sees a toy cookie, he may pretend to eat it instead of giving it to a doll to eat.

Continues to develop Object permanence.

Demonstrates tool use to obtain a desired object. For instance, he will use a stick to get a toy.

How does this relate to the language of a seventeen-to-nineteen-month-old child?

True verbal language begins—yay!

Vocabulary grows, and words can be used to express various functions.

Language is used to talk about the here and now and not *absent situations*. At this stage of development, the child cannot be expected to answer the question, "What did you do at Grandma's house?"

Stage 4: Nineteen to twenty-two months old

Extends symbolism to others, which means the child will feed the doll a cookie, brush its hair, or try to do this to another child or person.

Combines two toys in play (e.g., a bottle and a doll).

How does this relate to the language of a nineteen-to-twenty-two-month-old child?

Word combinations emerge to express different meanings.

Use of the possessive *my* tends to predominate, especially when in a group setting (e.g., "my doll," "my car," "my ball").

Objects and persons not present can be mentioned and talked about.

Morphological endings such as -s, -ed, and -ing are not yet produced.

Stage 5: Twenty-four months old

Participates in pretend play routines that represent daily activities. For instance, the child plays house by pretending to be Mommy or Daddy.

❖ There are no true sequences of events in the play, and the objects involved must be realistic in size and appearance. For instance, the child will pretend to cook using a play kitchen set, but he will not necessarily play with the kitchen set in a dollhouse.

Will stack and knock down blocks but not yet build representational structures, such as a house, a bed, or a train when playing with blocks.

Will fill and dump containers when playing with sand and water but not yet build representation structures, such as sand castles.

How does this relate to the language of a twenty-four-month-old child?

The child uses short sentences to describe his actions.

Present progressive: -ing tense, plurals, and possessive words are emerging.

Stage 6: Two and a half years old

Begins to represent events that he has experienced or observed infrequently in his life. These events tend to be memorable because they may be traumatic in nature, such as going to the doctor's office or going to school.

Parallel play occurs most of the time, but associative play is emerging.

❖ Parallel play is when children play alongside each other but the play is independent and not interactive in nature. They are participating in a similar activity, but their toys are not intermingling.

❖ Associative play occurs when a group of children participate in similar activities (like playing on the playground) but do not act together to follow directions or work toward a specific goal.

How does this relate to the language of a two-and-a-half-year-old child?

The child starts to use language to analyze situations.

Questions such as what, who, where, and why begin to emerge. However, even though the child asks "why" questions, he may not listen to the answer!

Stage 7: Three years old

Continues to engage in pretend play, but the sequences become more complicated and follow more steps. For instance, the child pretends to bake cookies by mixing them, baking them, serving and eating them, and then washing the dishes.

More associative play develops, but it is not yet cooperative play.

❖ Cooperative play occurs when children participate in a more organized, planned fashion and are working together for a purpose (e.g., using a play kitchen and pretending to cook food).

How does this relate to the language of a three-year-old child?

Since the child now understands more sequencing of events, he is able to better comprehend the concept of past events. Thus, more past-tense verbs are starting to emerge, such as "walked" and "ate." Earlier than this, the child may have used the past tense to mark a *change in state* rather than using it to mark the meaning of something that happened in the past. A *change in state* means that some action took place to make something change (e.g., "broke," "fell," or "opened").

Stage 8: Three to three and a half years old

Pretend play evolves into symbolic pretend play because the child now has the basis to understand that play can be used with less realistic toys. This is when children really start to have fun playing with dollhouses and toy characters. They begin to use objects to make representations (a row of blocks becomes trees in a forest or represents cars on a road).

How does this relate to the language of a three- to three-and-a-half-year-old child?

There is a considerable increase in descriptive vocabulary because the child perceives a greater number of differences and similarities between and among objects.

There is an increase in dialogue and narration of play. The child may say the stuffed animal is sleeping in his bed, or has a tummy ache and needs to see a doctor.

Appendix E

Common First Words

Here's a list of common first words. This list has been adapted from *The Rossetti Infant Toddler Language Scale* (2006). For our purposes, I have categorized the words by nouns (person, places, or things), verbs (action words), adjectives (attributes or describing words), and other. The "other" category includes possessives, prepositions, greetings, etc.

If your child is not yet using these words, try to target some words from this list during the activities presented in this book.

Nouns (Person, Place or Thing):

Apple	Car	Ears	Mama/Mommy	Spoon
Arms	Cat/Kitty	Eyes	Milk	Stick
Baby	Chair	Feet	Mouth	Stove
Ball	Cheese	Fingers	Nose	Teeth
Balloon	Choo-choo	Flowers	Paper	Toes
Banana	Church	Girl	Phone	Toy
Bear (teddy)	Clock	Grandma	Pizza	Truck
Belly/Tummy	Coat	Grandpa	Potty	TV
Bike	Comb	Gum	Purse	You
Bird	Cookie	Hair	Rock	
Book	Cracker	Hands	Shirt	
Boots	Cup	Hat	Shoe	
Boy	Dada/Daddy	Horse/horsey	Sky	
Bug	Diaper	Hot dog	Sleep	
Bunny	Dog/Doggie	Key	Snow	
Candy	Drink	Legs	Sock	

Verbs (Action Words):

Done	Eat (eat cookie)	Put	Sleep	Want
Drink	Fall (fall down)	See	Snow	
Comb	Go (go bed, go bye-bye, go night-night, go out, go potty)	Sit (sit down)	Swing	

Adjectives (Attributes or Describing Words):

Big (so big)	Dirty	Little	Thirsty	Wet
Cold	Hot	Old	Tired	Yucky

Other Forms:

These may include greetings ("Hi!"), requests ("please"), possession ("mine"), quantity ("all"), animal sounds ("moo"), rejection ("No!"), or prepositions (words that mark location).

All (all gone)	Huh?	Moo	Quack-quack
Bye/bye-bye	I	More	Shhh
Don't	In	Neigh Neigh	Thank you
Done	On	No	Uh-oh
Down	Out	On	Up
Here	Me	Out	What?
Hi	Mine	Put	What's that?

Appendix F

Language Goals

The following are some simple language goals that may help to guide your efforts. If your toddler is not yet talking, select a reasonable starting goal and build from that point. Feel free to adapt or change the goal to suit your needs. Consult a speech-language pathologist if you have genuine concerns about your child's speech and language, as they can help select appropriate goals and devise a treatment plan.

Receptive
(what the child will understand or follow):

The toddler will show word comprehension by looking at, picking up, or pointing to a named object or picture.

The toddler will identify named items by pointing.

The toddler will follow one-step directions (throw the ball, wash your hands, pick up the carrot) during a play routine and daily routines.

The toddler will follow two- and three-step directions (sit down and throw the ball, wash your hands and give me the towel) during his routines.

The toddler will understand prepositions such as *on, in, under,* and *next to* (put the ball *in* the basket, put the ball *on* the couch, put the ball *next to* the basket).

Other: _____

Expressive
(what the toddler will verbalize or say):

The toddler will imitate animal sounds when playing.

The toddler will imitate sounds and single words when playing.

The toddler will request help when needed ("Help," "Help me," "Help me, please," "I need help, please").

The toddler will use one or two words to express his needs and wants.

The toddler will name items on request or when prompted by an adult or another child ("water," "hippo," "a cat.").

The toddler will use one to two words to comment on objects and actions ("big ball," "nice dog," "dirty hands").

The toddler will use verbs ("run," "wash," "go") to narrate his actions or the actions of others.

Other: _____

Appendix G

Progress Chart

If you are interested in tracking what happens during certain activities or routines, you can record the results of your efforts with this chart.

Date:			
Activity/Daily Routine:			
Goal:			
Techniques Used:			
Results:			

Pocket Guides: Tips to Go!

Language Modeling Techniques & Elicitation Strategies

<u>Self-talk</u>

Talk about what you are doing, seeing, eating, touching, or thinking when your child is present. Narrate your actions - for example, "I'm washing the dishes. Now, I'm drying them. All done. I washed the dishes."

<u>Parallel talk</u>

Talk about what the child is doing, seeing, eating, or touching. In other words, narrate what he is doing - for example, "Now Johnny's washing the dishes. He's washing the plate. There, it's clean! All done. Johnny washed the plate."

<u>Expand</u>

Add grammatically correct information to your child's meaningful yet incomplete utterances. If your child says, "boy run," you could say, "Yes, the boy is running." Add in the missing words.

<u>Follow the toddler's lead in conversation</u>

Talk about what your child wants to talk about. If your child is looking at the rain, talk about the rain; if he is looking at the dog, talk about the dog. Acknowledge the child's words, phrases, and actions by saying something or doing something. Model or copy his actions, and then repeat and restate what he says. Be responsive to what he does or says, even if it's not a real word.

<u>Question a little, not a lot</u>

Don't inundate your child with too many questions. Remember to balance questions with comments. As a rule of thumb, saying at least three comments before asking one question is usually the best method.

<u>Pause in anticipation</u>

Wait approximately three to five seconds to give your child a chance to respond to what you have asked or said. Show that you are waiting expectantly by raising your eyebrows, smiling, and opening your mouth.

Sentence-completion tasks

This technique is best suited for older children, or those who have stronger comprehension skills. Try pairing verbal cues with visual or tactile input. For example, while giving him his shirt, say, "Here's your shirt. Put on your _____." Additional prompting may include use of phonemic cues. A phonemic cue is when you give the first sound of the target word. They help children retrieve words and say them quicker. For example, while giving him his shirt, say, "Here's your shirt. Put on your sh_____."

Choices

Give the toddler choices: "Do you want to eat crackers or grapes?" or "Do you want the cow or the horse?" Doing so puts indirect pressure on the toddler by presenting him with a concrete choice.

Oops!

Forget something essential or skip an important step in a routine. Most toddlers know when a routine has been violated and like to point it out.

Gestures, pantomime, or silly sounds

Use these to help the child understand your intentions. If you want his or her stuffed duck, make the quack-quack motion with your hands (four fingers come together to touch the thumb) while saying "quack quack."

Set it up

Set up a scenario so that the child has to ask for help or assistance. Give him a box or bag you know he can't open, or give him a task you know he will struggle with, so that he will have to ask for your help.

Troubleshooting Tips: What to Do if the Toddler Is Not Imitating You?

Remember **_R-A-I-S-E-S_** to help you facilitate your toddler's language learning by incorporating some of the following techniques into your play routines:

_R_educe pressure

Minimize the pressure you place on the toddler. Have you been asking too many questions? If so, replace a question with a comment. Instead of saying, "What is this?" while pointing to a picture, talk about what you see in the picture: "I see a big ball." Pause and look at the child. This way you are not confronting the child with a direct question or placing too many demands on him. Keep the play fun and lighthearted if you sense he has started to lose interest or get frustrated.

_A_dd support

Provide verbal, visual, and tactile (touch) support when needed. Show pictures, point to desired items, use gestures, and amplify sounds and words. For amplification, try using a microphone, a tube, or cardboard roll.

_I_mitate the child

If the child says "woof woof," echo it back to him: "woof woof." This strengthens the connection between the child and adult, and children often get very excited when adults imitate them!

_S_low it down

Slow down your rate of speech. Toddlers who are beginning to acquire language may not process what you are saying if you say it too quickly. Imagine trying to learn a new language with a teacher who speaks a mile a minute. It's pretty challenging.

_E_xaggerate your intonation

Slow down your rate of speech and use over-exaggerated intonation: "I reeeeeally liiiiiiike this game!"

_S_hort and sweet

I've mentioned this before, but it's worth repeating since I've seen many parents speak at a level above their toddler's abilities. If the child is only imitating one word when you say two or three, then do not produce a long-winded five- or six-word sentence with the expectation that the child will repeat a targeted word, because he has already forgotten what you said!

The Do Not List

Think *C-U-T-I-E* to help you remember what NOT to do while playing with *your* cutie!

Correcting your child's communication

For example, if your child is pointing to a dog and saying "daw," he should not be corrected by saying, "No, Johnny, that's a dog." For a child who has not begun talking yet, saying "daw" is a good improvement. Encourage and praise any attempts, even if they are weak or unintelligible, by repeating the desired target ("dog!") or praising his attempt: "You're right, Johnny, that's a dog!"

Using too many negatives

Avoid too many *no's* and *don'ts*. Plain and simple—negativity is not fun!

Teaching the ABCs

If the child is having a slow start in acquiring language, then I don't recommend teaching academically related vocabulary such as numbers, colors, letters, or shapes. It's better to target words that will give meaning and relevancy to his speech; this includes word categories such as actions, objects, locations, and attributes that are most relevant to a child's communication system.

Ignoring your child's interest

If your child points to a tree, look at the tree, acknowledge it, and say something about it or expand on what your child said about the tree. Don't begin talking about the weather or the neighbors. Stick to the topic!

Expecting too much too soon

Acquiring language is a process for some children. Toddlers are young and therefore need lots of opportunities, multiple contexts, and much repetition to acquire new skills. Some toddlers pick up words quickly, while others may take a more gradual approach. Give them time to grow at their own pace. Enjoy this playtime with your toddler, and make sure he feels that you are enjoying it, too, that it's not work or a chore. Toddlers are very perceptive and can tell when others are disappointed.

Some More Tips: The Five Rs

Here are five more tips to help accelerate your toddler's language learning.

*R*aise it up!

Hold desired objects or toys next to your face so that your child has to look at your face when you're talking. Placement next to your eyes or mouth is fine. For instance, if your toddler wants a cookie, hold the cookie close to your mouth while you say "cookie" so he can watch your lips move.

*R*einforce

Use natural reinforcers or rewards, such as giving your child a big hug, an extra turn in play, or verbal praise to keep him encouraged.

*R*espond

If your child said "ba" while pointing to a boat, acknowledge his verbal production by looking at the boat and talking about it. He is interested in that boat, which is why he tried to name it.

*R*earrange

Manipulate the environment to provide opportunities for communicating with preferred toys or everyday objects. Position favorite toys or desired objects in sight but out of reach. If you know he wants the fire truck because he plays with it every time he's in his highchair, do not just give it to him. Allow him the opportunity to point to the fire truck and try to name it before readily giving it to him. If he can't say it that's OK, just provide a model question, such as "Fire truck?" or "Do you want the fire truck?" Doing this will give him the opportunity to verbalize his needs and wants.

*R*elax and wait…a little

Give the child enough time to explore and problem solve. Toddlers learn through discovery. Provide them with just enough support so that they can try to figure it out on their own. Try to gauge or anticipate when you need to help them so that they don't get frustrated. How do you know an activity is too challenging or advanced for the child? If the child becomes frustrated, then this may be a sign that he is over-taxed or simply not understanding it. Stop the activity or make it easier if you find that the child is no longer having fun.

Notes

References

Bergen, Doris. "Pretend Play and Young Children's Development." *ERIC Digest* EDO-PS-01-10 (2001). <u>http://ceep.crc.uiuc.edu/eecearchive/digests/2001/bergen01.pdf</u>.

DeThorne, L. S., C. J. Johnson, L. Walder, & J. Mahurin-Smith. "When 'Simon Says' Doesn't Work: Alternatives to Imitation for Facilitating Early Speech Development." *American Journal of Speech-Language Pathology* 18 (2009), 133–145.

Donahue-Kilburg, G. *Family-Centered Early Intervention for Communication Disorders.* Gaithersburg: Aspen Publishers, Inc, 1992.

Ginsburg, K. "The Importance of Play in Promoting Healthy Child Development and Maintaining Strong Parent-Child Bonds." *Pediatrics* 119, no. 1 (2007): 182–191.

Hoff, E. *Language Development* (3rd ed.). Belmont: Thomson Wadworth (2005).

Paul, R. *Language Disorders from Infancy through Adolescence* (2nd ed.). St. Louis: Mosby, Inc., 2001.

Rossetti, L. *The Rossetti Infant-Toddler Language Scale: A Measure of Communication and Interaction.* East Moline: Linguisystems, Inc., 2006.

Westby, C. E. "The Westby Play Scale: Assessment of Cognitive and Language Abilities through Play. *Language, Speech, and Hearing Services in Schools,* 11 (1980): 154–68.